LUNCH LINES
silly riddles for lunchtime giggles

by Dan Signer

illustrated by Robert Shadbolt

chronicle books · san francisco

Text © 2011 by Dan Signer.
Illustrations © 2011 by Chronicle Books LLC.

Barbie is a trademark of Mattel, Inc.
Spider-Man is a trademark of Marvel Characters, Inc.
Starbucks is a trademark of Starbucks Corporation.
Tinkerbell is a trademark of Disney.
Yoda is a trademark of Lucas Licensing Ltd.
Porsche is a trademark of Porsche Cars North America, Inc.
Scope is a trademark of Procter & Gamble.

ISBN: 978-0-8118-7639-1

The illustrations in this book were digitally rendered.

Manufactured in China.

20 19 18 17 16 15 14 13

Chronicle Books LLC
680 Second Street, San Francisco, California 94107
www.chroniclekids.com

The Story of Lunch Lines

When my son Benny started school and I discovered I had to make his lunch every day, I thought it would be nice to include a little note. And I figured, why not a little joke?

So, I began writing jokes . . . and more jokes . . . wow, there are a lot of school days in the year. I started to look forward to the days he stayed home sick. Okay, not really.

Benny started reading the jokes to his friends during the lunch break at school. Soon he was reading them to the entire class. Before long, other teachers and the principal would come by at lunch to hear "Benny's joke."

Every night at dinner, I'd ask Benny what that day's joke had been. He always remembered it word for word. Then he'd tell me why it was funny.

By the time summer break (mercifully) rolled around, I was staring at a shoebox stuffed with jokes. (Benny saved them all.) And the idea for *Lunch Lines* was born.

How to Use *Lunch Lines*

Lunch Lines contains 188 individual tear-out jokes—enough for every school day in a year. Each day, simply tear out one page and fold it into a little card with the setup (question) of the joke on the outside and the punch line (answer) on the inside, and stick it in your child's lunchbox.

What do you
call someone
who designs dog
houses?

(front of card)

A
<u>bark-itect</u>.

(inside of card)

Plus, there's blank space on the inside of each card to write an optional personal note to your child—"I love you," or "Good luck on your quiz," or "Eat your carrots!"

The jokes in this book are on a range of kid-friendly topics, using familiar words, concepts, and references. But some will challenge your kids a little, helping to expand their knowledge, sharpen their comprehension abilities, and improve their reading skills.

Each night, ask your child to tell you (or read you) that day's joke. You can explain why it's funny, if needed. But most of the time, your child will explain it to you!

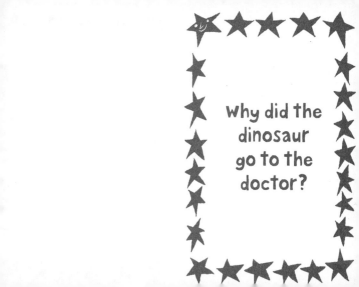

Why did the dinosaur go to the doctor?

He was
feeling
jura-<u>sick</u>.

What game
do fish like
to play?

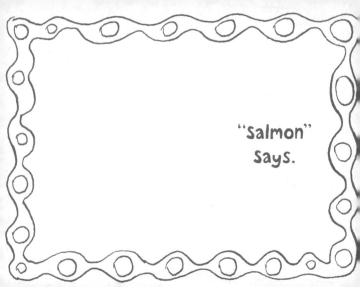

"Salmon" Says.

what's sweet, round, and deadly?

A
tae-kwon
do-nut.

What do you call someone who designs dog houses?

A
<u>bark</u>-itect.

what
kind of
cookies
do trolls
eat?

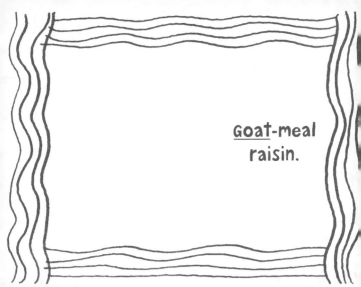

<u>Goat</u>-meal
raisin.

what do
frogs eat
with their
hamburgers?

French
"flies."

Why did the mastodon get sent to the principal's office?

PRINCIPAL

Because he was a "bully" mammoth.

what is
Baby Beluga's
favorite
song?

"The Whales on the Bus."

what does
a sneezing
ballerina
wear?

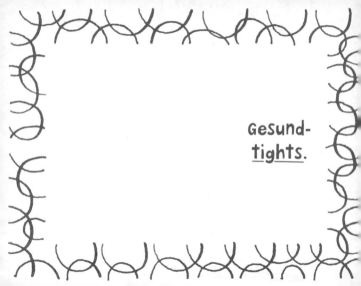

Gesund-
<u>tights.</u>

what doll
likes to grill
meat?

Barbie-que.

What did the termites do when they went to a restaurant?

They asked for a table for two... then they ate it.

what is a
pirate's
favorite
school
activity?

"Arrrrrts" and crafts.

What cleans
the floor and
then comes
back to you?

A <u>broom</u>-erang.

What kind of music do birds like?

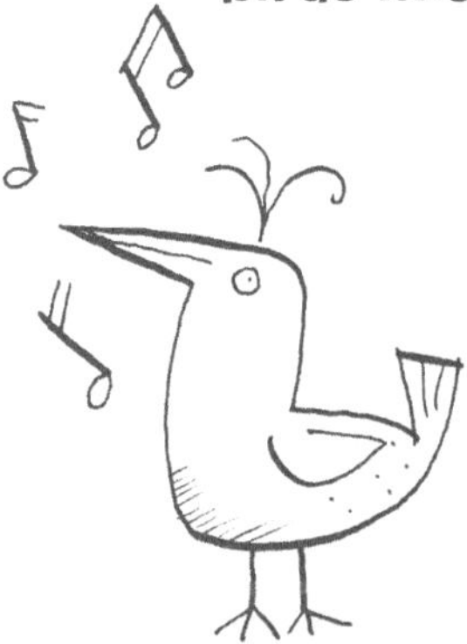

"Squawk"
and roll.

Why was
the ice
cream
lonely?

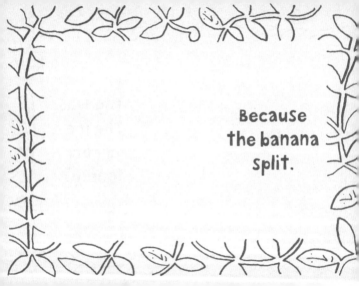

Because
the banana
split.

what's
dead and
buzzes?

A zom-<u>bee</u>.

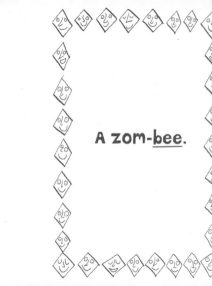

what do police use to arrest pigs?

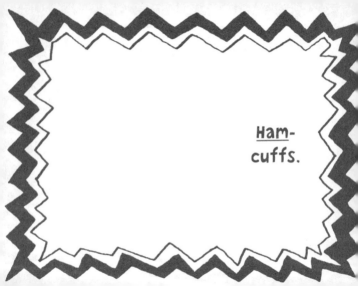

Ham-
cuffs.

what did
one volcano
say to
the other
volcano?

"I <u>lava</u> you."

what kind
of monkey
floats?

A hot-air
"baboon."

How much
salt do
crabs put
on their
food?

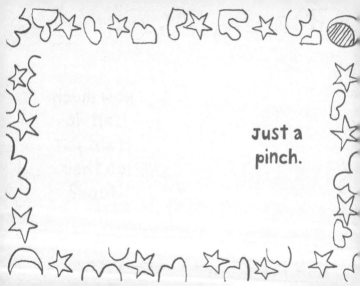

Just a
pinch.

what do
carnivores
eat in
space?

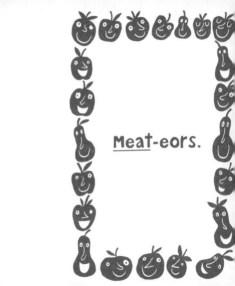

Meat-eors.

what makes a
baby go up,
down, and
loop-de-loop?

A "stroller" coaster.

What do you call a sleeping cow?

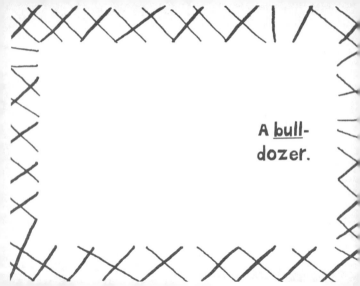

A <u>bull</u>-
dozer.

what do you
get when
you burn a
bagel?

<u>Holey</u>
smoke.

What do you get when you cross a legendary water creature with a criminal?

The Loch
Ness
"mobster."

Why did the cactus giggle?

Because it
was <u>prick</u>-lish.

what does
a lion use
to check
its hair?

A mir-<u>roar</u>.

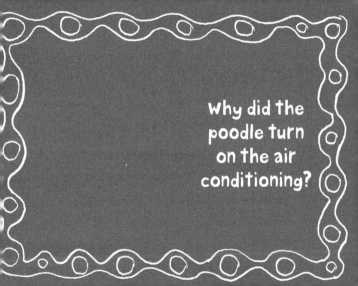

Why did the poodle turn on the air conditioning?

So she
wouldn't
be a
hot dog.

Search
the Web.

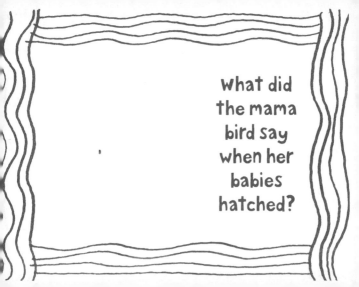

what did
the mama
bird say
when her
babies
hatched?

"Flappy birthday!"

what do
Olympic
runners use
to check
their
e-mail?

The
<u>sprinter</u>-net.

what
do swamp
creatures
eat for
dessert?

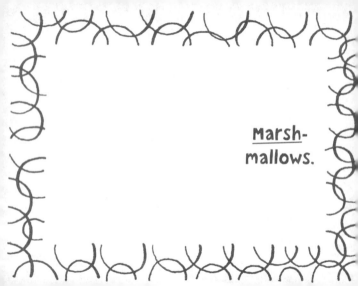

Marsh-
mallows.

What kind
of fish fixes
musical
instruments?

Why did the baseball player leave the stadium?

His coach
told him to
run home.

How
does the
ocean say
hello?

It doesn't.
It just
waves.

what
insect goes
well with
jelly?

A peanut
butterfly.

What does
Tinkerbell
sit on?

Her
fairy
tail.

Why should you never invite an aardvark to your family reunion?

Because
it will eat
all your
"aunts."

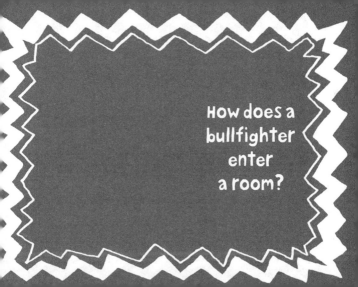

How does a bullfighter enter a room?

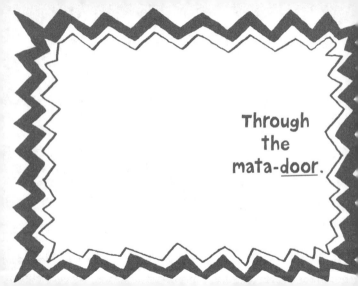

Through
the
mata-<u>door</u>.

where do fish
buy their
groceries?

At the <u>grouper</u>-market.

What do you call a 90-year-old woman who eats porridge?

oldie-
locks.

where
do bees
go when
they're
sick?

To the <u>wasp</u>-ital.

Why did
the train
engineer
choke?

He forgot to
"choo-choo"
his food.

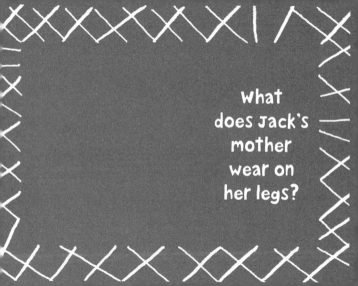

what
does Jack's
mother
wear on
her legs?

Bean
"stockings."

what has
stripes
and eats
bananas?

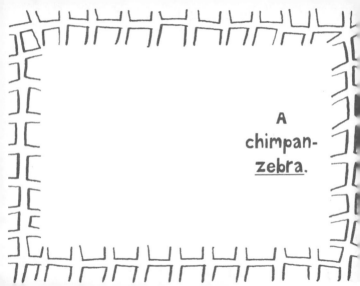

A
chimpan-
<u>zebra</u>.

what did
the mitten
say to
the hand?

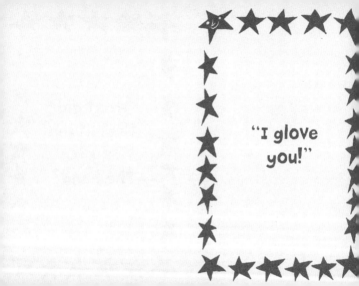

"I glove you!"

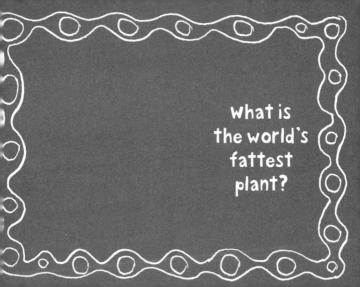

what is
the world's
fattest
plant?

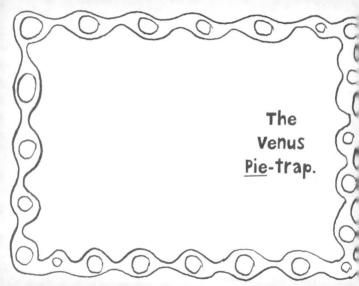

The
Venus
<u>Pie</u>-trap.

why did
the police
officer bring
a blanket
to work?

Because the chief told him to go "under cover."

Why did the
mermaid
buy a
computer?

So she
could
check her
<u>sea</u>-mail.

why did the
rooster buy
mittens?

So his
chicken
fingers
wouldn't
get cold.

Why did the rabbit open a barbershop?

She
wanted
to be a
"hare"
stylist.

what is
cold,
delicious,
and goes up
and down?

Frozen
yo-yogurt.

How do
wealthy beans
get around
town?

They ride in
a <u>lima</u>-sine.

where do
phantoms
go to mail
letters?

The "ghost" office.

what did
the salad
say to the
croutons?

"Lettuce
be friends."

What do
hip-hop
singers
put on a
birthday
present?

"Rapping" paper.

What do you
call a secret
agent that
weighs 2,000
pounds and hides
in the mud?

A
<u>Spy</u>-noceros.

Why didn't
the queen
believe her
husband?

Because he was the "Lyin' King."

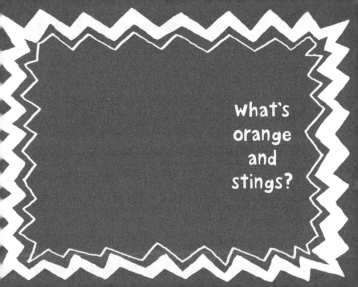

What's orange and stings?

Macaroni
and "bees."

Why did the
archaeologist
quit her job?

She didn't
dig it.

where
do baby
cows eat?

In the <u>calf</u>-eteria.

what did
the soup
say to the
pot?

where do
dogs drive
their cars?

on the
<u>flea</u>-way.

what
covered the
Yellow
Brick Road
with snow?

The "blizzard" of oz.

what's a butterfly's favorite school subject?

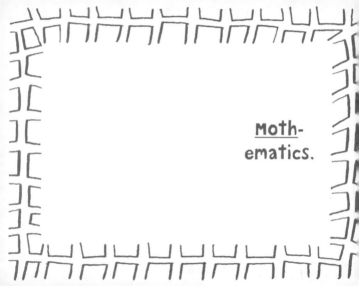

Moth-
ematics.

what has four
wheels and a
trunk but doesn't
need gas?

An elephant
on a
skateboard.

Why don't turkeys make good pitchers?

They
always
throw
"fowl"
balls.

what
does a
dinosaur
sit on?

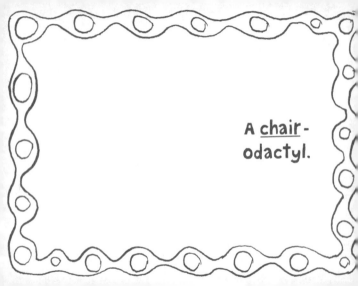

A <u>chair</u>-odactyl.

Why did the
mountain
fall in love
with the
canyon?

Because
it was
<u>gorge</u>-ous.

what does a ghost use to fly in the sky?

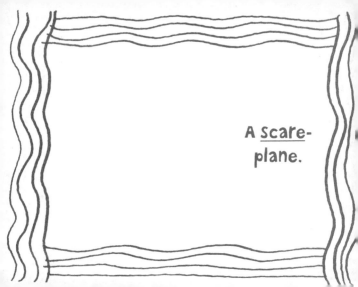

A <u>scare</u>-
plane.

What do you call a watch with eight hands?

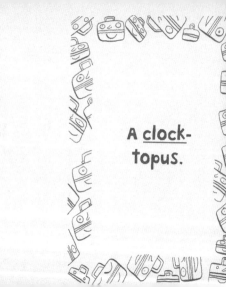

A <u>clock</u>-topus.

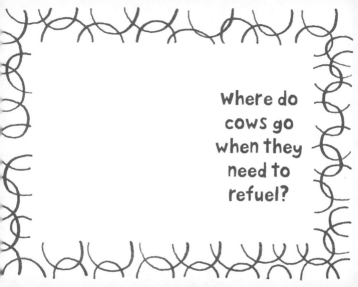

Where do cows go when they need to refuel?

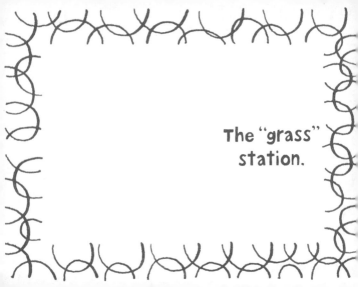

The "grass"
station.

what kind
of money do
aliens use?

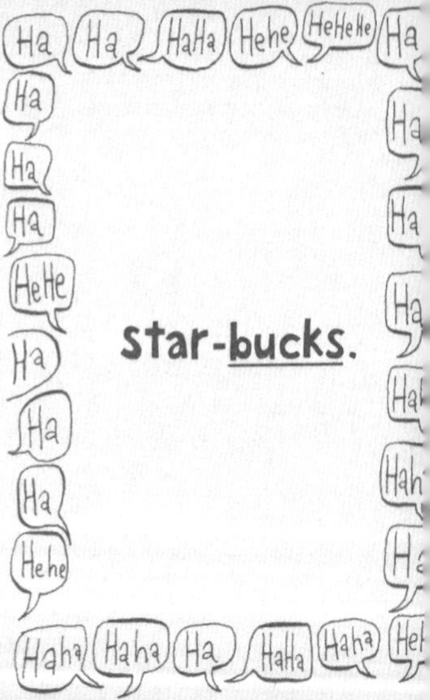
Ha
Ha
HaHa
Hehe
HeHeHe
Ha
Ha
Ha
Ha
HeHe
Ha
Ha
Ha
Hehe
Haha
Haha
Ha
HaHa
Haha
Ha
Ha
Ha

star-bucks.

Why couldn't the
cat play on
the computer?

Because she
ate the mouse.

what
growls as
it floats
to the
ground?

A <u>bear</u>-
achute.

Why
couldn't
the fish
talk?

He was sea "hoarse."

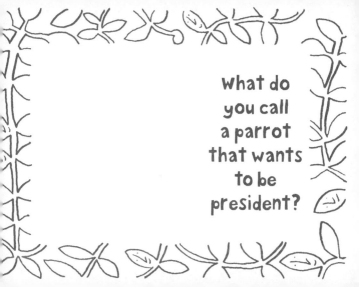

what do
you call
a parrot
that wants
to be
president?

A <u>Polly</u>-
tician.

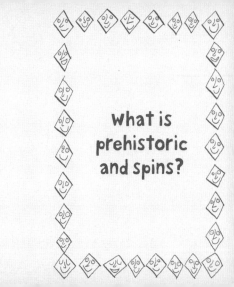

what is
prehistoric
and spins?

A tricera-
top.

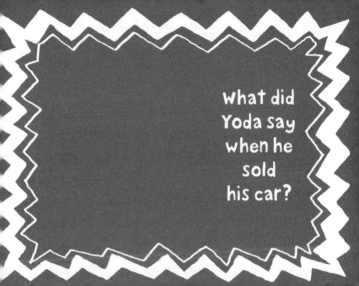

What did Yoda say when he sold his car?

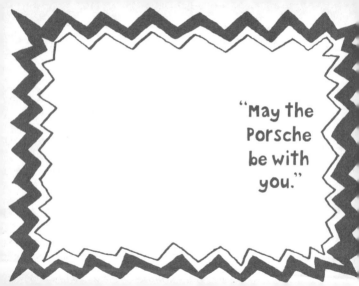

"May the Porsche be with you."

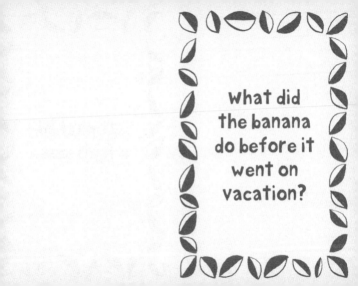

What did
the banana
do before it
went on
vacation?

It packed
a <u>fruit</u>-case.

what is a
sheep's
favorite
karate
move?

A lamb
chop.

what did the
electrician
say when
he got hurt
on the job?

Nothing.
He was too
shocked.

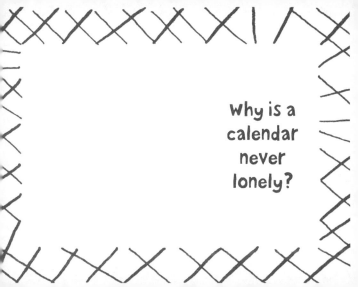

Why is a
calendar
never
lonely?

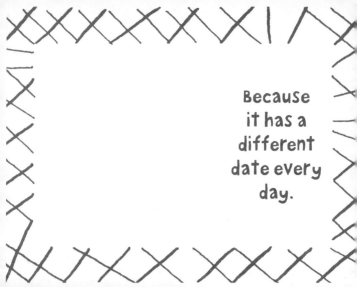

Because it has a different date every day.

Why did the piglets fall asleep in school?

Their teacher
was a real
"boar."

what did
the tree
say to the
squirrel?

Why did the forgetful man go for a run?

He was
trying to
jog his
memory.

What dessert slithers down your throat?

A <u>pie</u>-thon.

what is a
fish's
favorite
planet?

Nep-<u>tuna</u>.

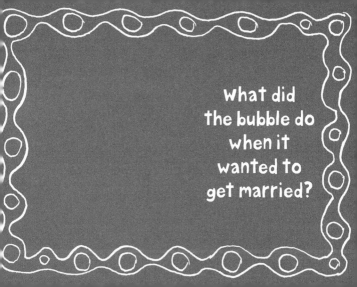

What did the bubble do when it wanted to get married?

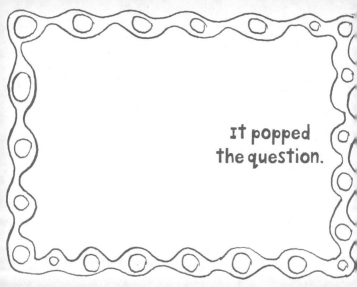

It popped
the question.

what
musical
instrument
do skeletons
play?

The
trom-<u>bone</u>.

HOW do you get a bison to fly?

Give him
some buffalo
wings.

What's
messy and
lives in
the ocean?

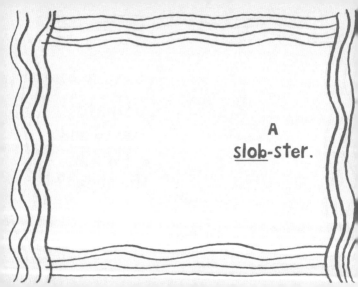

A
<u>slob</u>-ster.

what state
can you
write with?

Pencil-
vania.

Why should you never tell a secret to a piñata?

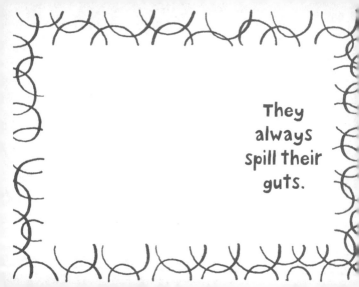

They
always
spill their
guts.

Why did the
farmer put
a bandage
on his goat?

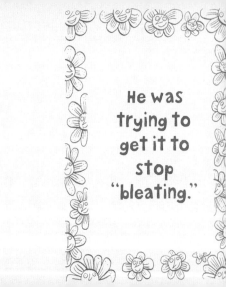

He was
trying to
get it to
stop
"bleating."

Why did
the bucket
bounce?

Because it
was filled
with spring
water.

what do mermaids use to wash their hair?

What did
Old McDonald
say when
he stepped
on his rake?

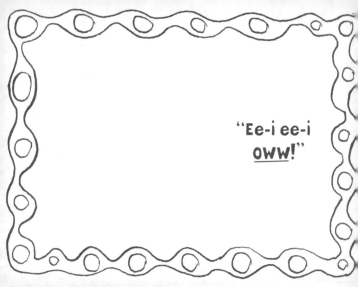

"Ee-i ee-i
<u>oww!</u>"

what is
a baker's
favorite
fairy tale?

Beauty
and the
"Yeast."

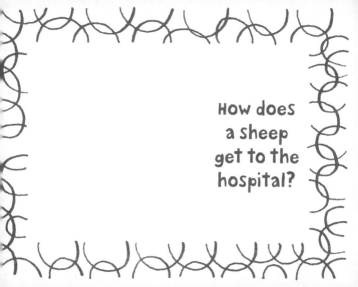

How does
a sheep
get to the
hospital?

By <u>lamb-bulance</u>.

Why did
the chicken
play guitar?

Because someone ate her drumsticks.

What does
Dracula
say when
you give him
a present?

"Fang
you very
much."

what do
you call a
prehistoric cat
that lives next
door to you?

A <u>neighbor</u>-
toothed tiger.

what is
the world's
richest nut?

The
<u>cash-ew</u>.

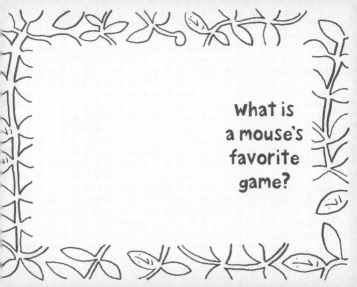

what is
a mouse's
favorite
game?

Hide-
and-
squeak.

what did
the dinosaur
say when
she hurt
her leg?

"My ankle-
is-<u>soreus</u>."

What does
a butterfly
sleep on?

A cater-
<u>pillow</u>.

what do
you feed
a cat
from outer
space?

A flying
saucer
of milk.

Why did the actor buy toilet paper?

He wanted
to get
a "role."

what is a
cheerleader's
favorite
fruit?

A
<u>pom-pom-</u>
egranate.

what does
a gorilla
use to open
a door?

A mon-<u>key</u>.

what do
planets do
when they
get dirty?

They take
a meteor
shower.

How do
you say
good-bye
to a math
teacher?

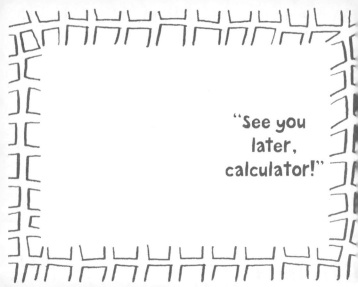

"See you later, calculator!"

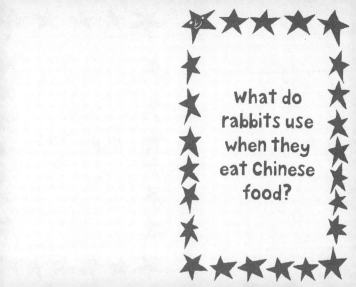

what do
rabbits use
when they
eat Chinese
food?

<u>HOp</u>-sticks.

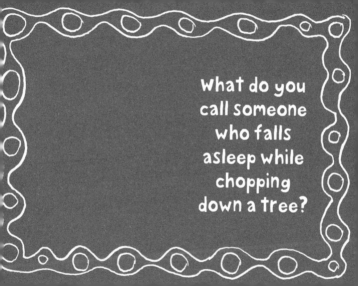

What do you call someone who falls asleep while chopping down a tree?

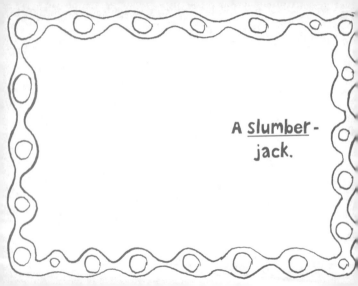

A <u>slumber</u>-
jack.

where can
you see
videos of
ghosts?

on
<u>Boo</u>-Tube.

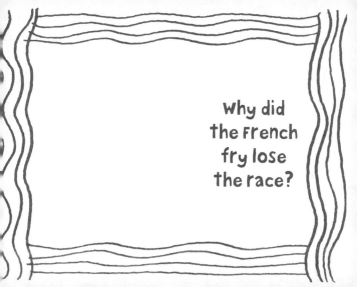

Why did
the french
fry lose
the race?

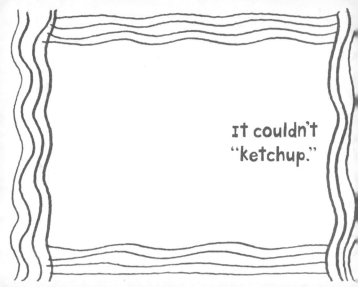

what do you call a pig that jingles?

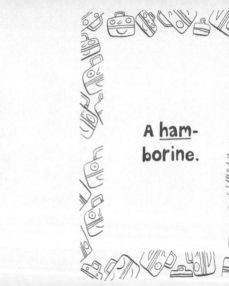

A <u>ham</u>-
borine.

what did
the boy
lizard say
to the
girl lizard?

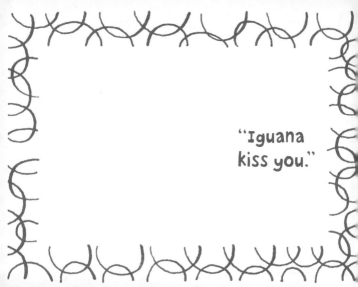

"Iguana
kiss you."

what kind
of lightbulbs
do wolves
use?

Howl-ogen.

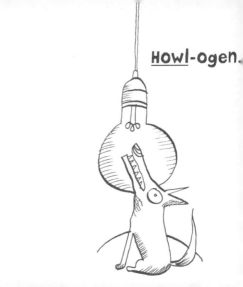

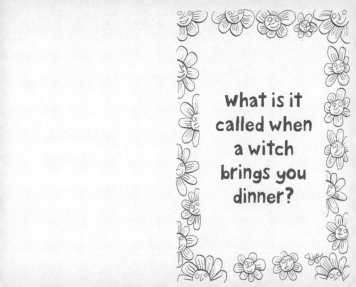

what is it
called when
a witch
brings you
dinner?

"Broom" service.

Why is the
ocean so
strong?

Because
it has a
lot of
"mussels."

what movie is about a bouncing dog?

Why did the bucket go to the doctor?

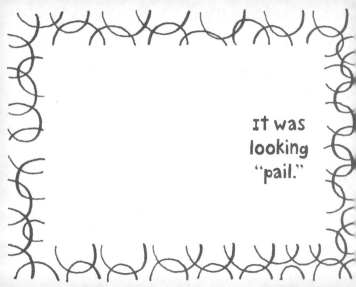

It was
looking
"pail."

what do
you call a
horse that
lives on your
street?

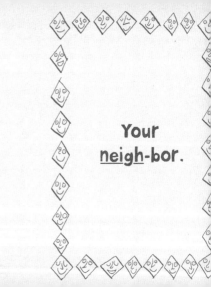

Your
<u>neigh</u>-bor.

what do
cats do
when they
join a
monastery?

They take a "meow" of silence.

Why did
the rope
get a
time-out?

Because
it was very
"knotty."

what has
antlers and
drinks blood?

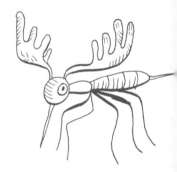

A <u>moose</u>-quito.

What is a
camel's
favorite
nursery
rhyme?

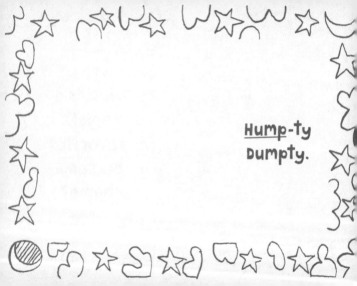

Hump-ty
Dumpty.

what time
do chickens
wake up?

Seven o'<u>cluck</u>.

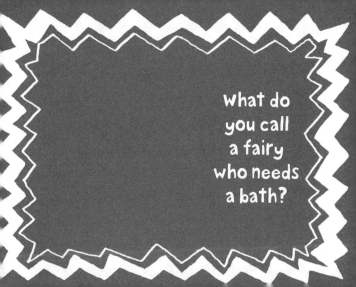

what do you call a fairy who needs a bath?

<u>stinker</u>-bell.

where do
pigs leave
their cars?

In a "porking" lot.

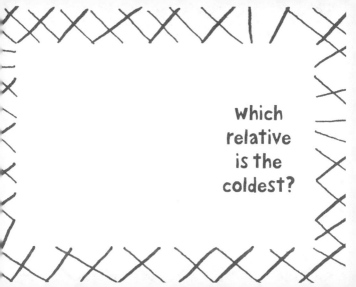

Which
relative
is the
coldest?

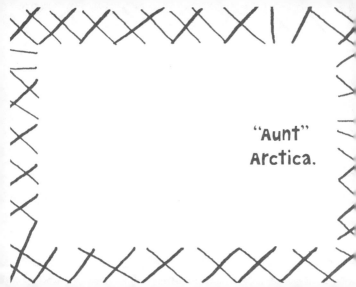

"Aunt"
Arctica.

How do
you put a
skeleton
to sleep?

Sing it a
<u>skull</u>-aby.

What song did the mommy oyster sing to the baby oyster?

"Mary Had
a Little
clam."

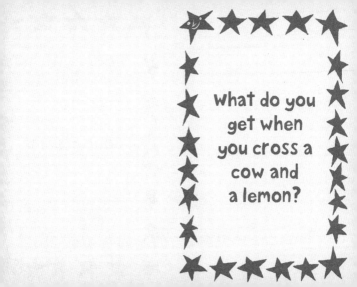

what do you
get when
you cross a
cow and
a lemon?

Sour cream.

which
planet is
the richest?

Saturn,
because it has
so many rings.

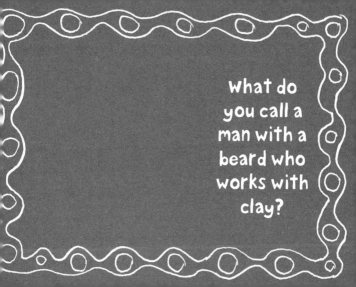

What do you call a man with a beard who works with clay?

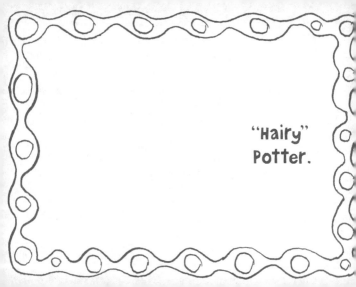

"Hairy"
Potter.

what do
policemen
eat for
dessert?

"Cop" cakes.

Why did the
skyscraper
write a
book?

Because
it had so
many
stories.

Did you hear about the restaurant for people with no teeth?

It's called "The Mush-Room."

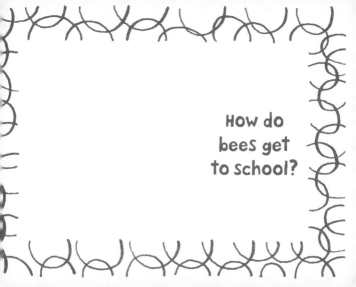

How do
bees get
to school?

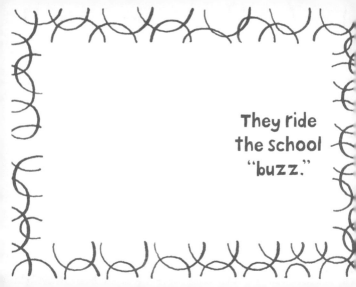

They ride
the school
"buzz."

What does
a tree wear
once it is
potty-
trained?

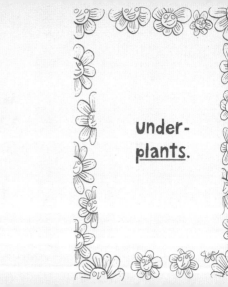

under-
<u>plants</u>.

where can
you find a
barbershop
for lions?

on "Mane"
Street.

what does a
cavewoman
wear when
she gets
chilly?

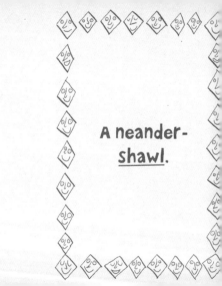

A neander-
<u>shawl.</u>

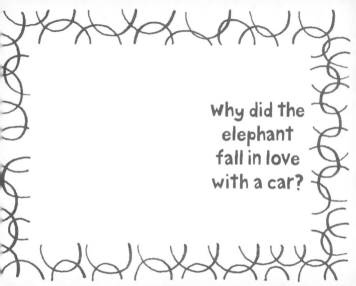

Why did the
elephant
fall in love
with a car?

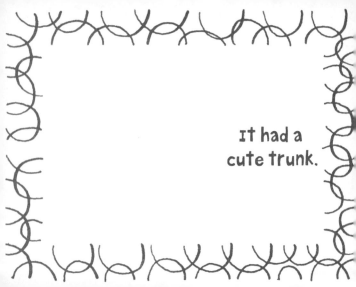

It had a
cute trunk.

What do you give a dinosaur with bad eyesight?

Tyrannosaurus "specs."

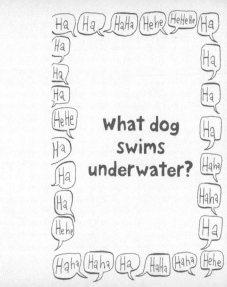

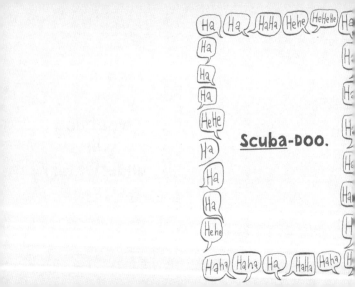

Why did
the shirt
go to the
doctor?

It was
feeling
"blousy."

What did
the umpire
say when
he wanted
pancakes?

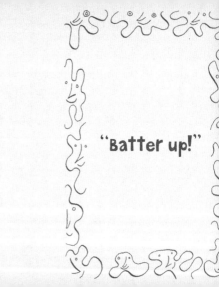

"Batter up!"

what's prickly
and flies?

A <u>stork</u>-upine.

Where do
cows eat
popcorn?

At the <u>moo</u>-vie theater.

Why did
the musical
group
bounce?

Because
they were
a <u>rubber-
band</u>.

what do you call 500 cats flying through the air?

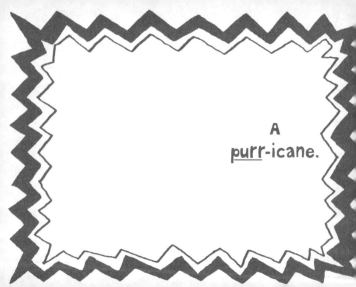

A
<u>purr</u>-icane.

what kind
of car does
a wasp
drive?

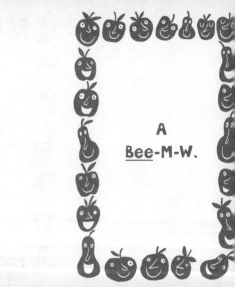

A
<u>Bee-M-W.</u>

What's
the laziest
food?

Bread.
It likes to
"loaf"
around.

what does
a gorilla
wear when
it cooks?

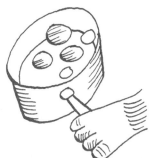

An ape-ron.

what is
a frog's
favorite
soda?

Croak-
a-cola.

What do you call a vampire who likes to eat between meals?

Count
<u>Snackula.</u>

What do you feed a squirrel from outer space?

Astro-<u>nuts</u>.

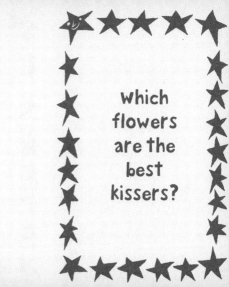

which
flowers
are the
best
kissers?

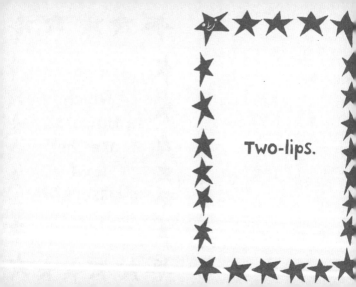

Two-lips.

How do snails start their bedtime stories?

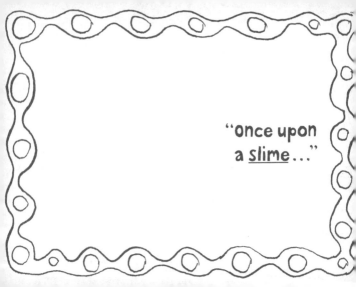

"Once upon a <u>slime</u>…"

Why did the girl put lipstick on her math quiz?

Because the teacher said it was a "make-up" test.

what do
you call
a toilet
that plays
music?

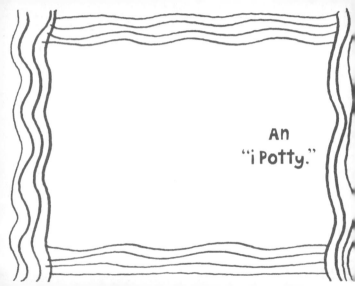

An
"i Potty."

what do
basketball
players
sleep in?

"Dunk"
beds.

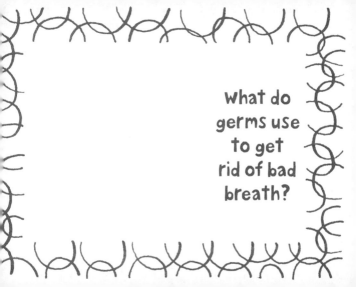

what do
germs use
to get
rid of bad
breath?

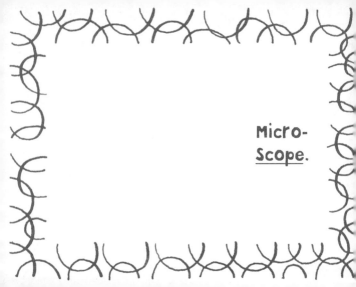

Micro-
Scope.

what sound
does a
prehistoric
dog make?

Jurassic
"Bark."

Why didn't the shark apologize for splashing the dolphin?

Because he
did it on
"porpoise."

Why did the marathon runner stop to buy lettuce?

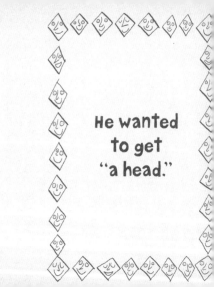

He wanted
to get
"a head."

What's the scariest kind of wood?

Bam-<u>BOO</u>!

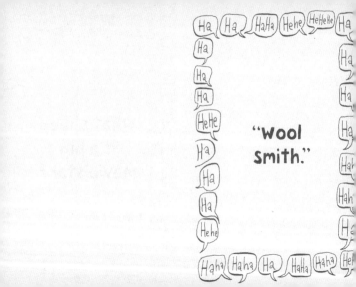

what do you call someone who pretends to play an instrument?

A saxo-
<u>phony</u>.

Why did the
boy bring
a skunk to
school?

For
show and
"smell."

what does
a snowman
wear when
he goes for
a ride?

An "icicle"
helmet.

what do
monsters
put on
bagels?

"Scream"
cheese.

what goes
well with
milk and
squeaks
when you
bite into it?

A chocolate "chipmunk" cookie.

why
didn't the
roofer
have
a wife?

Because
he was a
"shingle"
man.

why did the
stegosaurus
apologize?

Because
he was
dino-<u>sorry</u>.

What do you call 100 centipedes?

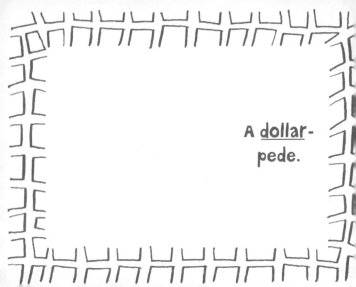

A <u>dollar</u>-pede.

Why did
the river
read the
newspaper?

It wanted
to keep up
on "current"
events.

what does
a shrimp do
if he can't
drive?

He takes a
taxi "crab."

what do chickens do when they break their legs?

They
get an
<u>eggs</u>-ray.

what did
the mommy
snake give
the baby
snake?

A
goodnight
"hiss."

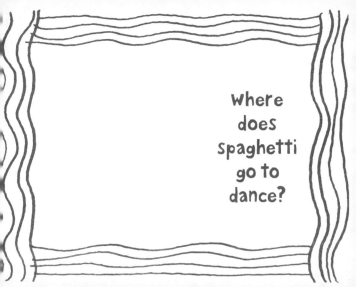

where
does
spaghetti
go to
dance?

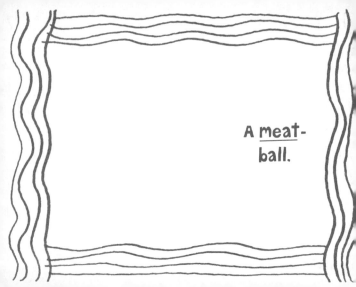

A meat-
ball.

Why did
the dog
meow?

He was
just
"kitten"
around.

What did
the gymnast
do when
she won a
gold medal?

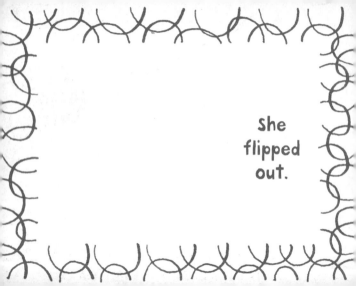

She
flipped
out.